Deep in the Sea

By Liza Charlesworth

ISBN: 978-1-339-02795-1

Art Director: Tannaz Fassihi; Designer: Tanya Chernyak
Photos ©: p5 Krill: Tarpan/Shutterstock.com. All other photos © Getty Images.
Copyright © Liza Charlesworth. All rights reserved. Published by Scholastic Inc.

1 2 3 4 5 6 7 8 9 10 68 32 31 30 29 28 27 26 25 24 23

Printed in Jiaxing, China. First printing, August 2023.

SCHOLASTIC

The sea is huge and deep.
It's wide with white foam.
Let's dive in and take a peek
beneath the waves!

This reef is beneath the waves.
A reef is a home for bright fish.
They flash and glide!

A humpback whale is in the sea.
When it swims, it flaps its fins
and slaps its tail. Whack!
It can go 100 miles in a day!

krill

crab

This fish is an eel.
It is long and thin like a snake.
Eels hide in the holes of reefs.
They feast on krill and crabs.

In the sea, seals flip and play.

Crabs creep on rocks.

Rays seem to fly!

In the sea, green plants sway.

You might spot a huge clam!

You might spot a pink snail!

Can you spot a man? Yes!
He dove deep into the sea
to take snapshots of fish.
Swim, glide, flash, swish!